I0159430

Stop Drinking: *Continue the Journey*

Let's start with 21 days...
By Kuda Midzi

Copyright © 2017 by Kuda Midzi
All rights reserved. This book or any portion thereof
may not be reproduced or used in any manner
whatsoever without the express written permission of
the publisher except for the use of brief quotations in a
book review.

Printed in Canada

First Printing, 2017

ISBN 978-0-9959397-0-7

Contents

Introduction

My name is Kuda Midzi and I hope my journey to sobriety helps you continue with yours. I say continue, because this isn't the first time many of us have thought about getting sober. If we've failed before, we ask ourselves why we should keep trying. The fear of failure keeps us from pushing on, but I'll show you why you need to stop trying and just commit to getting sober. As long as you are using the word *try*, you are ready to accept either outcome.

This book is not just for alcoholics. I'm here to help anyone living with addiction and a gut feeling that it's time to break free of it. Whether you've been called an alcoholic or addict by others, or you have labelled yourself, there comes a point in your life when you consider quitting. Your intentions may have been good, but you became sidetracked and returned to your vice. My focus is to help as many of you break that vicious cycle, as I possibly can.

I faced the added challenge of being a parent who could not afford rehab, and needed to continue working to support my family. I felt trapped despite my desire to quit. I was aware of the negative health effects caused by drinking, and I expect you are too. I will not waste words discussing alcohol's ill effects, because this information does not deter most addicts anyway. I will focus more on the real reason why you are reading this, and that is to get sober once and for all. To get there just remember…

**You don't have to be sober to get started;
you have to get started to become sober.**

I made the necessary commitment, followed a few simple steps, and in May of 2012 I achieved my goal. Now 5 years sober, I strongly believe that following the few ideas I outline in this book will help you overcome addiction. At the end of each chapter I will ask you to answer a question, and provide blank space for you to write notes that resonate with you. Writing things down often helps you remember what your intended plan is.

The Pain of Discipline

Making the decision to stop and wanting to change was the easiest part of the journey. Although I had tried and failed many times over, I still knew one day I'd have to stop for good. I decided to reflect and be honest with myself. How would I conquer this mountain? I honestly saw no way I could achieve this goal. My heart wanted to stop, but my mind told me I couldn't. I made half-hearted commitments to sobriety, by drinking less or quitting only one of my regular beverages. I was half-hearted because I didn't really believe sobriety was possible after so many failed attempts. "Why should I even try?" I would often ask myself.

I always hoped and prayed that one day I would stop. Sometimes I prayed out of remorse. Spending too much on liquor, or wasting a day with a terrible headache were among my regrets. Friends and family always saw potential in me that I was wasting; they told me I could do great things (they just never said what). My successful journey began when I established a pattern of praying every Sunday, to be forgiven for what I'd done over the weekend. Many times I'd heard, "You cannot expect things to change when you keep doing the same thing." I came to terms with the fact that trying to lessen my drinking would not help me quit. My weakness was getting a paycheque in hand, as I always found a reason to buy drinks. A few drinks led to hard liquor, and inevitable drunkenness ensued.

One day I decided to thank the Lord for the life I had, rather than asking to be forgiven for something I didn't even remember. I always knew that the Lord loved me, because he brought me out every situation alive and protected me from what could have happened. Many times I knew just how bad things could have easily gone, which led to a form of depression. If you're at the end of your rope and ready to give sobriety one more try, ask the Lord to free you of your addiction. Immediately be thankful that you are coming out. Once your heart and mind are aligned things will happen.

Things you've heard before will take on new meaning, because the words are meant for you now. I heard Joel Osteen talk about how to start a new habit. His plan only took 21 days, so I decided to test it. "Why not?" I asked myself. To be honest, at the start I was not convinced that I could do it (especially with smoking as an added hurdle). The first day was probably the easiest, because I was still fired up. I didn't tell anyone what I was doing for the first couple days, because I didn't know what would happen. The challenge came on day two, when my cravings seemed to have doubled. It was then that I heard Joel Osteen say,

"The pain of discipline is minuscule compared to the pain of regret."

It was around day nine or ten that I decided to start marking my calendar every morning. All I would do was tick off the day, so I could see how many days had gone by without smoking or drinking. It was my secret at the start, because I still had doubts in the back of my head. The visual representation of my progress took a weight off my shoulders and increased my confidence. I further reinforced my strength by listening to faith-building messages.

I didn't need to record my progress for long, as by around day 15 I had abandoned my calendar. By that point I knew I had conquered the battle and felt unexplainable confidence. I knew I'd won when I stopped trying. I told myself, "I'm done." As long as you are *trying* there is a chance of failure. When you are *doing* it is for a specific outcome (in this case, freedom from addiction).

Once I had acknowledged that it was my time for freedom, my worry was considerably reduced. I found solace in the passage from God, where he promises, "grace for the day." All I had to do was not drink or smoke for one day, then do the same thing everyday thereafter. Friday was still a challenge, so I gave myself an extra dose of encouragement. I liked playing pool, and realized I could have just as much fun doing it sober. The greatest rewards came when I woke up in the morning. I knew how much money I had, no one was mad at me, and I didn't have to fear what I might have done the night before.

Waking up completely sober on Saturday morning makes it easier to get through the weekend, because your day is not spoiled. You just have to hold on for Saturday, and when Sunday comes you are still sober. Now you have a resting day for the week. Remember that you prayed once for strength and thanked the Lord that you are free; just stay thankful as you encounter temptation. Many provinces have a lot of liquor and beer stores, so you'll likely have to pass them. You will inevitably be tempted more and more, but that's when you celebrate inside. When the temptation is greatest, you are closest to your miracle. You've made it through one more day.

You can also look at your journey from the perspective that in 21 days you will either be drinking or sober. It's simply up to you to decide what state you'll be in. You will have to find your own coping mechanisms, because time will never stop. It's up to you to use time wisely to arrive at your destiny. I urge you to self-reflect and see if you really want to reach your goal. If I can do it, you can too.

Today is ———————————— , ————————

and I have decided to start my 21 day challenge.

These are the things I am going to change:

1. _____

2. _____

3. _____

This is my commitment to get through 21 days and continue my journey. I will take it one day at a time.

Notes to Myself: _____

_____

_____

_____

_____

_____

_____

_____

_____

_____

Your Journey with Loved Ones

One of the biggest challenges in this journey is facing your family and friends. It is very hard to convince them that you're changing, because you may have disappointed them multiple times when you said you would stop in the past. They may have even offered their help before, but have since given up on you. People can only be disappointed so many times before they make up their mind to move on.

Family

When I decided to start my 21-day trial, I did not tell anyone. I think this was wise in the early stages. When I tried to tell people that I was quitting after several attempts, I could tell they didn't believe me – their reactions said it all. I had genuinely tried to stop for the sake of my family, among other reasons. My motivations were never strong enough to make quitting seem possible though.

My siblings had also tried to help by encouraging me to quit, pray, and go to church. None of their persuasions had worked though. Sometimes, after lasting a week I would gladly announce that I was okay. When the weekend came around though, I was drunk again and calling them pretending to be sober. They all saw through me, and this cycle went on for years. I have many more miserable stories to tell, but they are not the purpose of this book.

Convincing my family that I was going to quit was not an option for me for two reasons: I still had to convince myself, and they knew me too well to believe me. They frequently reminded me how bad alcohol was for my health, and that it would kill me one day. Many people who drink know about the harmful effects already, and eventually become blind to the warnings that are all around them. What they say is no secret to you, but they keep trying in the hope that one day you'll listen. My family knew most of my failures were caused by alcohol, and they reminded me of this.

I started my journey in secret, because I could not handle negativity in my fragile state. You feel pain and tremendous self-doubt when someone you love and trust asks, "What makes this time any different than the many times you've said this before?" There is no need to raise peoples' hopes. For me their body language and voice said it all. After talking to them I didn't see the point in trying. I called myself a failure, and turned back to drinking. It's funny to consider that as an alcoholic you drink for joy, sadness, anger, stress, or just about any other emotion.

When you are seriously committed to your journey, you often learn things about yourself. I never knew I could be disciplined, resourceful, or stand up for myself. Many people now tell me that I have strong willpower. What they don't understand is how much time it took me to develop that. The more days I went without drinking, the easier it got and my confidence grew. Willpower is a developed ability, which is not merely engrained from birth. The more days, weeks and months that go by, the more your family will notice a difference in you. They'll see the improvement in how you carry yourself and interact with them.

Some alcoholics argue that no one can judge them because they don't know their story. They blame their built-up anger and unresolved issues for driving them to drink. I say it does not matter what the cause is when you want to stop. All that matters is what you are doing about it. Clearly drinking doesn't solve your problems, it merely delays you having to think about them.

What if your family members know which buttons to press to make you angry? I've heard of 1 to a box theory, which reminds us that some people might not support you, because they fear their own failure. If you succeed, they may feel left behind. Others' insecurities don't matter though, you just have to run your own race. Know that this is an individual journey, and it's up to you determine the results.

What if your family and friends are drinking and having fun around you? Not everyone is going to be happy about your changes, mainly because they couldn't do it themselves. We all have our own reasons to stop; you thought about stopping and that's reason enough. We often hope and pray for our big dreams to come true. Just imagine the Lord saying, "Do you want your big dreams to come to pass? These are the sacrifices you have to make."

What if you are not in a good place or healthy environment right now? Quickly changing your environment does not necessarily help with addiction. No matter where you are, you are still attracted to the idea of drinking and will look for similar places to get your fix. Just continue your journey where you are right now. The way you see things will change as time goes by, and if necessary you will move in time.

Do you have an abusive spouse or family member? One thing everyone has to know, is that you can't really change other people. If someone else's behaviour is driving you to drink, I have a few ideas you can try. Please note that I am not a doctor nor licensed professional, I'm merely someone who's been in your shoes and can speak from experience. I advise you to pray with faith for the changes that you want, and believe it's working in the outside realm. Dig deep and see why you are still there. Are you still there for the right reasons, or has your self-worth been compromised? Who were you before, and who are you now? Is it worth it to stay, or are you settling for a mediocre life? Only you can answer those questions. Once you have answered those questions, evaluate and make a decision to gradually change your life, whether you maintain your relationships or not. Either way, action has to be taken, because taking no action is a conscious decision to stay in the same situation.

When your family finally knows you have broken through, they'll say they were rooting for you all along (despite their lack of faith). LOL. I have always appreciated my family's prayers throughout my journey.

Friends

Friends are awesome! They are your friends simply because you like doing similar things. I was very fortunate to have friends that didn't really push me to drink. Mostly I was secretive with them about my journey, because they thought it was only a matter of time before I dove back in. The first few weekends I would lie about why I wasn't drinking. Sometimes I would say I had no funds, drank too much and needed a break for the weekend, or had stomach problems. They would just laugh it off.

Though it may seem selfish, I'm glad I never tried to take friends with me on my journey. It was a big enough battle alone, without having to convince someone else to quit. Many people will think you're quitting because of a tragic event, but you can quit anytime and for any reason. What I found interesting, is that 90% of the time I met with my friends who were drinking, they said they envied my willpower to have fun sober. They would then go on about their attempts to quit, and some would even say they were sober for as much as 6 months until life hit them hard.

"I'm not an alcoholic and I can stop whenever I want," my friends would say right after sharing their failed attempts to quit. I never instigated conversations about whether alcohol is bad or not. I was just a man on a mission, and my mission statement was clear – STAY SOBER. I never really changed my friends, but they knew I didn't drink anymore and I became the designated driver. Many admired my courage, and it moved them because they knew me. Some secretly asked me how I did it, whether I was taking medication, and how I continued to be sober. Knowing me and how much I used to drink, they could not believe my journey was that simple.

I live by the notion that I can be the light for my friends, and that change is possible wherever you are. You do not need to move away from family or friends to start your journey. Just start where you are, and God will provide a way forward. You will be surprised to see that the friends you once worried about end up in your corner, once they see you are in it to win. It's only natural that your persistence will be tested, just don't be too quick to disqualify your own people. Many have secretly tried and failed, and they just want to see if you can do it. Also remember that you may have once been a disbelieving friend, when someone else was on their journey... you may have even been worse! LOL.

Mindset

It's one thing when it's your first time quitting, or you're going cold turkey, but there's a whole new set of challenges if you've tried and failed like I had. If this isn't your first battle, these words are for you: My commitment was to get through each day, but whether from bad habit or something happening at work, I felt I NEEDED a beer. Through the grace of our Lord I did not go for it, but my mind knew that it was only a matter of time before I caved. Many people might not understand this, but when you are doing the best you can within your human ability, strength finds you (e.g. someone says something to reignite your spirits). You have take all the good you can get, and never dismiss encouragement. When I was having tough thoughts I happened to listen to a message from Joel Osteen (I believe he was talking about something like mental toughness), and at that point I knew his message was for me. As I've said, you usually just need a push to get you through that day.

One thing I never thought to do, was turn away from my friends or the places I liked to go in the beginning. For whatever reason, I felt that I was the light for my friends. I did not shy away from any of them. I lived with one of my close friends, and when I told him I was taking a break from alcohol, he was happy that the expense was less. I still went to the liquor store with him, and bought him beer with my money. I just made sure I didn't buy it for myself as well. There is a great sense of accomplishment when you can go to a local store and not buy beer for yourself. You've avoided it not because you can't afford it, but just because you don't want it. I knew that running away from this challenge was not going to help me. Beer was everywhere I liked to hang out, so I had to face the music. There is no greater feeling than that of beating temptation. People will see you a little more joyful and not know why, but you will know inside. I decided to keep my quitting a secret so that I had less people to answer to. I don't know what it's called, but when you can retrain your mind to win daily battles, it becomes second nature and the battle is easier. The temptation does not go away, you just deal with it quicker. You'll find that instead of obsessing over how you are going to continue like this, your mind quickly turns to thinking about something like work or family.

When people talk about willpower and discipline, they often make the mistake of thinking you just have it in you. It's often forgotten that it has to be developed, and it may be painful because you are going against yourself. You will never know how much willpower you have until you test it and stay committed. Test the waters and you will see your true self.

Since I can only change myself, I will not put any effort into changing others. These are the major changes I am making to better myself.

1. _____

2. _____

3. _____

This is my personal journey, and I will start where I am. These are the people I may have to love from a distance:

1. _____

2. _____

3. _____

These were my excuses and I will commit to never using them again:

1. _____

2. _____

3. _____

4. _____

5. _____

Notes to Myself: _____

When it's Time it's Time

There comes a time for most of us, when we stop to think about our lives; where we are, where we have been and where we are going. The same thing happens when you drink. There is a point when the thought of quitting will cross your mind, most likely because you regret something. That thought crossing your mind is not the same as God putting an impression in your heart that it's time to stop. This is God telling you that a better life is available. You'll know this impression is true when it does not go away, and you think about it more often than you ever have before. Even if you have not been drinking for several days, what you feel in your heart won't go away.

One thing I really feared when God's impression kept coming was success. I often thought about what I would do if I stopped drinking, and what my friends would think. I often thought about the things I loved to do, like drink and play pool or snooker and watch UFC at bars. My battle was now fear of a boring life without alcohol, and I don't know why I thought that. I often thought drinking was the only way to have real fun. The first few beers where okay, but after a few I couldn't stop. I went from having fun to blacking out, and this was causing strife in my family. I believed that my plan was perfect when I started drinking on the weekend. I would drink a few then stop, but I always I ended up having way more than I planned. Regrets came the next day when I couldn't tell you how I managed to get home, or what had happened the previous night.

God put an impression in my heart long before I stopped. Now that I think about it, strife began to set in after I received the Lord's message. I started to drink a lot more and could not stop. Eventually in 2011 I was involved in a drinking and driving accident. I believe God caused that accident, because I walked away without a scratch and it was far less severe than it could have been. Although I was uninjured, the car was a write-off. My indiscipline led to God causing the accident. I thank the Lord for allowing this to happen, because it could have been so much worse. Nevertheless, it took me over a year to actually decide to stop drinking.

You will know deep down inside when it's time let go of your addiction, no matter what it is. Say yes to what your heart desires. Once you've accepted that you and the Lord are in agreement, it is possible. The first part of freeing yourself from drinking is to know and accept that it's time to stop.

There are some impressions that the Lord leaves you with that you simply can't shake off. These impressions have always been there, and do not have to relate to drinking. You may feel guided to help others, write a book, start a job that you love, travel to see a loved one, or be a better parent etc.

These are the impressions that keep coming at me:

1. _____

2. _____

3. _____

4. _____

5. _____

These are the plans I have for each one:

1. _____

2. _____

3. _____

4. _____

5. _____

Today is _____ , _____
and I will commit to take action toward realizing my impressions and gut feelings. I will continue to add more to this list as it comes.

Notes to Myself:

The Truth Shall Set You Free

Like the Bible says, (this is one of its most popular statements) *the truth shall set you free*. What is the truth? There is a great deal of information from scholarly studies on this topic. The truth is, you are greater than the addiction. The truth is that with the small pain of discipline, you can achieve all that you want. If you fall, rise up immediately rather than taking comfort in self-pity. You will never know the strength of your willpower until you test it. Forget trying to stop, and STOP for good. If you want to know if your are ready for your journey, start NOW and make tomorrow day one.

Your key to victory is to maintain discipline in times of temptation. Keep inspirational messages close to your heart. Many people cannot afford therapy or counselling, or are even ashamed of it. I was not taught or counselled, and I did not study for my journey. I simply made a few changes and persevered until the challenge became easier. Sometimes too much information can be overwhelming. People tend to know how difficult it is to stop, but not how simple it is. Just take it one day at a time.

Do not focus on your past failures – today is a new day. Dust yourself off and get going. Just remember no more room for excuses. If you are about to use the word BUT, you are making an excuse for yourself. You can be your greatest inspiration, and don't have to depend on anyone for encouragement. If someone encourages you that's great, but if they aren't supportive that's great too, because it gives you a chance to prove them wrong.

Do not do this for anyone else but yourself. When you arrive at your goal the people you wanted to prove yourself to will celebrate with you. Do not try to drag anyone along for your journey. Instead start alone, and if anyone wishes to join you, make it clear that you are in it to win. It's great to have someone to make you accountable. If no one is along with you however, that should not deter you from moving forward. When you help others you will be helping yourself too. Just be wary of arguments that may not help your cause, because you don't have to convince anyone but yourself.

The fear of change is very real and daunting. We have to conquer that fear to reach new heights. I recall the hardest days to avoid drinking were my birthday and Christmas, as well as my six-month and 1-year anniversaries of sobriety. I was so tempted to celebrate with just one beer. LOL. I knew that if I could do it for a year though, then all I had to do was start the next year with just one more day. This serves as an example that even after you successfully quit, temptation still comes along. The key is to win these small battles.

I have emphasised that you just need to win one day at a time. You will find that your instinct takes over, telling you where to go or what to do. Trust those instincts, because your gut feeling is there for a reason. Some things may not make sense in the moment, but trust that it will one day. In my case it was a long time before I realized why I did not abandon my friends or fear the places I used to go. Funny enough, I got most of my encouragement in the places I used to drink once I had proved myself. How did I prove myself? I was not on a mission to specifically prove myself, but in reminiscing I realize that it came as a result of my commitment. I used to frequent a bar called Jox in

Edmonton, where they knew me and what I liked to order. During my first weeks of sobriety the servers continued to ask if I wanted a Heineken. At times they even put a bottle on my table already open, which I would pay for and give to a friend. I switched to ordering Sprite, and eventually they started bringing me that instead. People will notice when you have changed. You will not have to convince anyone.

You can compare your journey to a plane ride. Once you've cleared customs, shown your ticket and boarded, it's up to you what kind of flight you'll have. If you've watched negative newscasts, you may spend the flight in fear of a crash, failed landing, or even explosion. You are in the same position when you wake on the first day of your journey to sobriety. It's inevitable to have negative thoughts, as there's any number of excuses you could use to justify failure. Instead start your journey tomorrow without playing into your fears, as they only serve to inhibit your life.

To further explore the airplane metaphor, you can compare sitting aboard awaiting take-off to getting ready for your day. You must face the day in some way, so you may as well get ready for work and go. Regardless of whether you were an early drinker or late drinker, (I use past tense because your journey starts today) the approach of your regular time is much like a flight attendant instructing you to fasten your seatbelt. You're told to buckle up, because ascending to a comfortable altitude means you have to defeat the negative forces that pull you down. It will be a shaky, bumpy and uncomfortable ride that seems to take forever, but your plane will suddenly level off for smooth gliding. This is just like going cold-turkey, as you'll have to hold on through feeling sick, angry and confused. Your body has grown accustomed to alcohol consumption, and you need to re-teach it that not consuming is normal.

These are the early stages, when you'll be relaxed and comfortable during smooth flight, but encounter turbulence warnings and have to fasten your seatbelt. Do not be alarmed. Along your journey you will get gut feelings to avoid going somewhere, or not to be with someone on a certain day. Listen to those gut feelings, as they help you avoid turbulence. Sometimes you will ignore your gut, and encounter tougher challenges as a result. Once you overcome those challenges you will have grown, but suffered unnecessarily. It can be scary to follow your intuition, because at times it means hurting people you love and respect. You just have to draw a line in the moment, and you will later gain the respect of the people you thought your were hurting. At the very least, do not let anyone else become an excuse for abandoning the journey you're on. It's scary to go through turbulence, but I've noticed that you never know how long it will last. It can be very shaky or mildly shaky, but it most consistently ends when you least expect it. The mild shakes tend to last longer, whereas the heavy ones often end quickly; therefore do not fear the hardest times, because they'll be over before you know it.

The Small Prayer that Yields Big Results

First and foremost, you do not have to be a Christian to say this prayer. You just have to believe that your journey has started, and that God will guide you through it.

> *Father I thank you for the impression you have left in my heart. I have ignored your message in the past, which has caused heartache and pain. I have tried and failed to do this on my own. I surrender this challenge to you. I accept your daily dose of grace, and thank you for bringing me out stronger than before. Amen*

Feel free to make this prayer your own. Add or edit elements to suit your personal situation. The lord is good, so things will start to change as you go. You know the end goal and the first steps, so start NOW. It's time to march on one day at a time. Do what you can, and let God do the rest.

I , _____ understand this will be a bumpy road and have prepared my mind for victory. No matter how strong the temptation, I will win this battle.

These are my bumpy times:

1. _____

2. _____

3. _____

4. _____

5. _____

This is how I will overcome the bumps:

1. _____

2. _____

3. _____

4. _____

5. _____

This is my race and I own it. I will not make excuses, because I am prepared. I am committed to see this through.

I will still be sober on _____ , _____
(five years from now)

Notes to Myself:

As the Journey Continues

As you continue your journey, simply start again. Do not over-complicate things by trying to find new ways to do it. You should not fear failure at this stage, because you've more than likely tried and failed anyway. Many are used to wondering, "What if I try and fail?" Instead ask yourself, **"What if I try and succeed?"** Now that you've found the confidence to start, consider what the bible says: *faith without action is dead.*

At this point I'm often told, "wow, you had really strong willpower." Remember though that I did not have it to begin with. You do not know who you really are until you get tested. Once you pass the first test the following ones may be stronger, but you will have greater confidence from your first success. I simply remember that missing out on one day or night of drinking won't be the end of me, so I can go without this time. As the days and weeks go by, you will notice that your crowd will start to change. You will automatically be drawn to different things, but still love your friends from a distance.

Once you hit the three or six month mark, the temptation to celebrate with a drink will come. All you have to do is carry on what you've been doing though, or it's all for nothing. If your family is the biggest challenge, then challenge them to make sure you don't drink, and tell them to do whatever it takes to stop you. Many people can help others, but can't help themselves, so why not make use of them?

Never make the mistake of thinking that people have forgotten the old you. You may be reminded of your old ways by those who know you (whether their intentions are good or not), but you must keep on fighting regardless. You don't have to fight every battle, especially when it comes to convincing others that alcohol is unhealthy. You'll often be lectured about not drinking, especially by drunks. LOL. Take in worthwhile advice and discard useless information, but be careful not to feed your mind garbage. You already know your friends and family, so be sure to control your conversations to avoid them getting out of hand.

You will earn respect once your resilience has been tested. If you still feel the need to please everybody in your circle, you'd better brace yourself for a big disappointment. Once you've taken steps toward your journey, you will see who is for you and who is against you. Distribute your energy accordingly, and you will find you're still driven to continue. Your gut feeling will lead you. Your gut feeling is like a GPS system. When it is quite you are on the right path, so fear not.

You should know that good things will happen to you too. I say this because many people are hit with the realities of life, and expect bad things to happen. The words that come out of your mouth are very important, because their meaning has real-life effects. It's always better to develop a good rapport by speaking positively, rather than focussing on the negativity you are trying to free yourself of. This does not mean complete absence of negative thoughts, as I for one experience them every day. Sometimes I'm under the weather, or simply wake up on the wrong side of the bed. Negativity can't be avoided, but what comes out of your mouth is key to your day. I remember telling myself that it was possible to get through the weekend, because I did it the weekend before. Always celebrate even your small victories, and you'll find the bigger ones come easier.

Make discipline a major force in your life. Recondition your mind, and never say your progress is too good to be true. If you say something it is bound to happen. Funny enough, it takes about the same amount of energy to have positive expectations, as it does to have negative ones. Positive thinking just seems so difficult when we're wired to expect failure.

Many will say they want to quit, but as Les Brown said, "Want shows up in conversation, expectation shows up in behaviour." If you're pumped up about quitting, but feel alone in your fight, what are you going to do? Your behaviour will show what you expect to happen. Many people want things to change, but few make it happen. One of the main differences between success and failure is discipline. Because you are in a situation, you will probably know that you don't have the discipline yet. How then can you start to discipline yourself? Simply remember…

You don't have to be disciplined to get started; you have to get started to become disciplined.

You don't have to wait for the stars to align to get started. Even if you fall a few times, make sure you learn from your mistakes, and get back up even stronger. One day your step will be different; you will be transformed. Many people forget that the right time may never come, because there is always an excuse to delay. In Luke 17: 11-19 the bible says, "They were healed as they went." If you are planning to make changes in your day-to-day life, you have to start somewhere. Changes take place as a result of action. Believing in something is the start, but that's not all it takes. Acting on your belief brings things together. As the Nike slogan says, **JUST DO IT**.

On _____ , _____
I will put my plan into action.

I am expecting to be sober and these will be my milestones:

On _____ , _____
I will finish my 21-day test.

On _____ , _____
I will be 3 months sober.

On _____ , _____
I will be 6 months sober.

On _____ , _____
I will be 1 year sober.

I, _____ am committed to
achieving my goals and will celebrate my victories.

Notes to Myself:

In Conclusion

You don't have to be sober to get started;
you have to get started to become sober.

No more excuses, just do it.
Stay Blessed and Stay Sober

www.ingramcontent.com/pod-product-compliance
Lightning Source LLC
Chambersburg PA
CBHW060646030426
42337CB00018B/3472

9 780099 593970